Seeking
an Annulment
with the Help of
Your Catholic Faith

Seeking
an Annulment
with the Help of
Your Catholic Faith

Lorene Hanley Duquin

Our Sunday Visitor Publishing Division
Our Sunday Visitor, Inc.
Huntington, Indiana 46750

Nihil Obstat:
Rev. Michael Heintz
Censor Librorum

Imprimatur:
✠ John M. D'Arcy
Bishop of Fort Wayne-South Bend
November 20, 2006

The *Nihil Obstat* and *Imprimatur* are official declarations that a book or pamphlet is free of doctrinal or moral error. No implication is contained therein that those who have granted the *Nihil Obstat* or *Imprimatur* agree with the contents, opinions, or statements expressed.

DEDICATION

To Barbara Wyse and Veronica Cavan,
who have been companions to many people on the journey
through the annulment process.

A woman divorces her husband because of alcoholism and abuse. She wonders if she can get an annulment.

A man asks if he can get an annulment because he married his ex-spouse in a Protestant ceremony.

A woman explains how her parents pressured her to marry because she was pregnant. She wonders if this would be grounds for an annulment.

A man fears that an annulment will make his children illegitimate.

A woman admits that she was too young and immature when she married. She wonders if this would be grounds for an annulment.

An elderly couple who married outside the Church was denied an annulment in the 1970s. They want to know if they can try again.

Over the past fifteen years, I have helped a lot of people who had questions about annulments. Some people wanted to marry in the Catholic Church, but couldn't because one or both parties were divorced. Some couples wed in other churches or before a Justice of the Peace, and wanted to make things right with the Catholic Church. Some had no intention of ever remarrying, but wanted spiritual and emotional closure that their divorce process did not provide.

> It is more from carelessness about truth than from intentionally lying that there is so much falsehood in the world.
> — SAMUEL JOHNSON
> ❦❧

In working with these people, I've discovered that most of them have strange misconceptions about Catholic annulments. They are victims of people who are quick to offer bad advice and spread incorrect information.

✦ A family member told one woman that she needed an annulment because she wouldn't be able to receive Communion once her divorce decree became final. *This is NOT true.*

- A cousin told another woman that an annulment costs thousands of dollars. *This is NOT true.*
- One man's friend insisted that you have to have connections in order to get an annulment. *This is NOT true.*
- A co-worker told another man that people who have been married for a long time can't get annulments. *This is NOT true.*

The Facts about Annulments

✧ An annulment does *not* cost thousands of dollars. The average fee in most dioceses ranges from $350 to $1,000, which covers about half of the actual costs of processing the annulment. The diocese subsidizes the rest.

✧ No one is ever rejected because of financial difficulties or inability to pay the full amount.

✧ An annulment does *not* have to be processed in Rome, and you *don't* need connections in order to obtain one.

✧ You must go through a civil divorce before you can begin the annulment process.

✧ Most cases take about twelve to eighteen months to process. Some will take longer if there are complications with the paperwork or delays in obtaining the testimony of witnesses. Some will take less time.

✧ The length of the marriage and the number of children are *not* factors in the annulment process.

✧ There is no quota system. Each case is processed on an individual basis.

✧ An annulment does *not* mean that there was never a loving relationship or a civil marriage that was recognized by the state.

✧ An annulment does *not* make the children illegitimate.

✧ If you were denied an annulment, it is possible to reopen your case with new grounds or new witnesses. Anyone who was denied an annulment before the 1983 Code of Canon Law changes were implemented (in the late 1980s) should look into the possibility of reopening his or her case.

- ✦ A fallen-away Catholic told one couple that the Catholic Church uses the pain of the annulment process to punish divorced people. *This is NOT true.*
- ✦ A self-proclaimed "expert" on Catholicism convinced another couple that annulments take five or ten years because all annulments are processed in Rome. *This is NOT true.*

Because of this kind of bad information, there are people who never explore the annulment process. There are people who are afraid of the annulment process. There are people who want to investigate the possibility of an annulment, but don't know where to start.

A healing process
Many people have told me that the annulment process has the potential for spiritual and emotional healing, in that it offers the opportunity to explore aspects of the relationship that were often ignored in the divorce process. It allows a person to reopen the wound caused by the divorce and let the poison drain out. It provides closure.

Divorce and Excommunication

A divorced person is *not* automatically excommunicated. Horror stories abound in which divorced people stay away from the Catholic Church because they think they are barred from receiving Communion. A divorced person can receive Communion and participate in all parish liturgies and ministries.

Problems arise when a divorced person without an annulment marries again in a civil ceremony or another church. The Catholic Church does not recognize the second marriage. In these situations, people can still attend Mass, belong to the parish, raise their children as Catholics, have a Catholic funeral, and be buried in a Catholic cemetery, but they are not supposed to receive Communion until their marriage situation is resolved. This is not intended as punishment or discrimination. It is an attempt to uphold the teachings of Jesus regarding divorce and remarriage. Once an annulment is granted, the couple is encouraged to have their marriage validated and begin receiving the sacraments again.

- One man told me the annulment process helped him move on with his life.
- A woman told me the annulment process helped her believe that her former marriage was never meant to be.
- A young couple said the annulment process helped them reconnect with God and the Catholic Church.
- An elderly couple said the annulment process helped them forgive themselves and others for past mistakes.

The purpose of this little book is to present some of the ways your Catholic faith can help you through the annulment process. It will help you explore the tough questions, mixed emotions, painful memories, and technical procedures. It will guide you through the paperwork and interviews and offer suggestions on what to say to family members and friends about the process. Finally, it will give you a spiritual framework that can bring you to new life and a deeper sense of inner peace.

CHAPTER 1

What Is a Church Annulment?

When a man and a woman enter into the Sacrament of Matrimony, the Church presumes that their marriage is an exclusive, lifelong union that exists for the good of both spouses and for the procreation and nurturing of children.

The bride and groom confer the Sacrament of Matrimony on each other when they profess their vows. They solemnly promise to be faithful to each other all the days of their lives. They promise to accept children. The priest or deacon serves as a witness who affirms their words of consent on behalf of God and the Church.

An annulment (or "decree of nullity," as it is officially called) is a declaration by the Catholic Church that when the marriage vows were exchanged, there was an impediment that prevented one or both partners from making a mature, lifelong commitment. It means that no matter how good the marriage looked on the surface, when the vows were exchanged, one or both partners did not enter into the union in the way that the Catholic Church understands marriage.

> The consent by which the spouses mutually give and receive one another is sealed by God himself. . . . If consent is lacking, there is no marriage.
> — *Catechism of the Catholic Church*, 1639, 1629
>
> ~❧~

The reason the Church has an annulment process is because it takes seriously the words of Jesus in the Gospels that prohibit divorce and remarriage:

> "But from the beginning of creation, 'God made them male and female.' 'For this reason a man shall leave his father and mother and be joined to his wife, and the two shall become one.' So they are no longer two but one. What therefore God has joined together, let not man put asunder."
> — Mk. 10:6-9

If, however, God did *not* join the couple together, the Church can recognize that there was no sacramental union.

Different than divorce

An annulment is not a "Catholic divorce." In fact, a Catholic annulment is completely different from the legal process you went through during your divorce.

+ The annulment process does not focus on the reasons the marriage ended. It looks at the factors that influenced the couple leading up to the time the vows were exchanged.
+ The annulment process is not adversarial. There is no confrontation.
+ The annulment process is not secular. It seeks to understand whether God joined the man and the woman in marriage.

Think of it as a soul-searching process involving prayer, reflection and spiritual insights. It allows you to look back on the ways your family influenced you, how you met your ex-spouse, your ex-spouse's family, your engagement and the events leading up to the wedding to determine whether you and your ex-spouse were capable of entering into what the Church recognizes as a valid marriage.

What constitutes validity?

+ Both parties must possess sufficient use of reason and a mature understanding of the matrimonial rights and responsibilities.
+ Both parties must assume the obligations of marriage without serious psychological impediments.
+ Both parties must consent without pressure or force.
+ Both parties must promise that this will be a permanent, lifelong union.
+ Both parties must promise to be faithful.
+ Both parties must be open to the possibility of children.
+ Both parties must be honest with no fraud or deceit involved.

If one or more of these elements are absent when the vows were exchanged, grounds for an annulment may exist. For example:

+ If a marriage lasted less than a year, it probably involved a lack of commitment or maturity.

- A history of psychological disorders, addictions, irresponsible behavior, or deviant activities may point to an inability to assume the obligations of marriage.
- If there was physical or emotional abuse, questions may be raised as to whether there was a true understanding of the marriage covenant.
- A marriage involving an out-of-wedlock pregnancy raises questions about whether both parties gave consent without pressure or force.
- If either person felt a need to get away from an abusive parent or a dysfunctional family, validity of consent may be questioned.
- Suppressed gay or lesbian tendencies may have surfaced.
- One or both parties may have lacked the ability to make sound judgments.
- There might have been hidden motives for marrying, such as the desire for citizenship, the desire to have a child, or the desire for financial stability.
- A grieving widow or widower may have married quickly in a misguided attempt to replace the deceased spouse.
- One or both parties may have had no desire to have children.
- There might have been no real commitment to be faithful.

> Facts do not cease to exist because they are ignored.
> — ALDOUS HUXLEY

If grounds for an annulment exist, the Church has not only the right but the responsibility to investigate the possibility of nullity. It is a matter of justice and truth.

The annulment process

The first step in the annulment process is to talk to your parish priest or call your Diocesan Marriage Tribunal (the administrative office of the diocese that deals with marriages). You will be given forms to complete. You will also be asked to write a personal history and supply names of people who can back up your story.

After you mail the information to the tribunal, you will be invited to a preliminary interview. Someone at the tribunal will go over your paperwork with you. The tribunal will begin its preliminary investigation. After all of the information is collected, the tribunal will determine whether you have grounds for an annulment. If it does not appear as if you have grounds, you will be told that you can reopen your case with new information at a later date.

If it is decided that grounds exist, your case will be accepted for the formal annulment process. A petition will be drawn up and you will meet with someone from the tribunal for what is called a formal hearing.

> The truth will make you free.
> — JOHN 8:32
>
>

If the tribunal recommends that the marriage should be annulled, your case will be sent to another tribunal for review. If the second court agrees with the first, the annulment is granted. If the second court disagrees, the case can go to Rome for a final determination, but this happens very rarely.

Marriages outside the Church

Canon Law stipulates that a Catholic must marry according to the rites of the Catholic Church in the presence of a bishop, priest, or deacon, with two witnesses. A Catholic can be married by a non-Catholic clergy person only if permission is arranged through the diocese. The Catholic Church does

---

Sorting Out the Situations

Here's a little recap of who has to go through a formal annulment process, and who does not, due to "Lack of Form."

The formal annulment process is pursued when:

- ✧ Two Catholics were married in a Catholic Church.
- ✧ A Catholic and Non-Catholic were married in a Catholic Church.
- ✧ A Catholic and Non-Catholic were married in Protestant Church with permission.
- ✧ Two Non-Catholics were married in a church or by a Justice of the Peace or some other civil authority.

"Lack of Form" applies when:

- ✧ A Catholic was married by a Justice of the Peace or some other civil authority.
- ✧ A Catholic was married in another faith without permission.

These cases do not need formal annulments.

---

not allow Catholics to be married by a Justice of the Peace or some other civil authority.

Catholics who wed in another faith community without permission, or in a civil ceremony, are often surprised to learn that they don't need to go through the annulment process because the Church never recognized the marriage in the first place. These cases are called "Lack of Form" because the tribunal only needs to verify that the couple did not marry according to Church law.

"I was married by a Justice of the Peace," one woman recalled. "All I needed was my baptismal certificate, my marriage certificate, my divorce decree, and a small fee. My pastor filled out the form and within a few weeks I had papers saying I could marry in the Catholic Church."

Non-Catholic marriages

Since the Catholic Church cannot set standards for non-Catholic marriages, the Church presumes that all non-Catholic marriages — even those that take place before a Justice of the Peace — are valid in the eyes of God. As a result, a divorced non-Catholic who wants to become a Catholic or marry a Catholic in the Church does not qualify for the shorter "Lack of Form" procedure and has to go through the formal annulment process.

Why bother?

Some people decide that going through the annulment process is not worth the time or the trouble. "I don't think God would want anyone who desires the sacraments to be turned away for the sake of a piece of paper," one man told me.

> Every time there are losses there are choices to be made. You choose to live your losses as passages to anger, blame, hatred, depression, and resentment, or you choose to let these losses be passages to something new, something wider, something deeper.
> — HENRI NOUWEN

Other people, who are willing to open themselves spiritually and emotionally, find that the annulment process can help in ways they never imagined. "The annulment process provides healing for those who have gone through a divorce," one woman explained. "It helped me to come to peace with the past."

Starting the process

One of the most frequent questions is: When is the best time to start the annulment process?

The Pauline and Petrine Privileges

There are provisions in Canon Law for annulling marriages if one or both of the spouses are not baptized.

- ✦ The Pauline Privilege was a way of dissolving marriage in the early Church when one spouse decided to be baptized and the other refused. In 1 Corinthians 7:12-14, St. Paul says it is all right for baptized and non-baptized spouses to remain together. If, however, the unbaptized spouse decides to leave the marriage, the baptized spouse will be free to remarry another baptized person.

- ✦ The Petrine Privilege is granted only by the Pope, who can dissolve the previous marriage of an unbaptized person so that this person can be baptized Catholic or marry a Catholic.

These cases are always handled through the Diocesan Marriage Tribunal, which decides whether you should go through the formal annulment process or through a Pauline or Petrine Privilege.

You cannot open your annulment case until your divorce is final. Some people begin writing the papers while they are going through the divorce or immediately after the divorce is granted because the information is fresh in their minds. Other people wait years before they begin because they need distance to fully comprehend what happened. The reality is that people start when they decide this is something they want to do.

QUESTIONS FOR REFLECTION

1. Why are you looking into the annulment process?
2. What misconceptions did you have about the annulment process?
3. What makes you think that your previous marriage might be invalid?

CHAPTER 2

Overcoming Fear

I'll never forget the woman who carried annulment papers in her purse for three years. She couldn't bear to put them away, but she couldn't bear to work on them. She was afraid of reopening old wounds.

Fear is one of the most common emotions expressed by people who are thinking about the annulment process. Fear drains your energy and distorts your perception of reality. It may be hard to believe, but most of the things you fear about the annulment process will never happen. Recent studies suggest that fear of pain is much worse than the pain itself. In the absence of fear, whatever pain you experience will be significantly less intense.

> He who fears he shall suffer, already suffers what he fears.
>
> — MICHEL DE MONTAIGNE
>
> ~€€~

Dealing with fear

The first step in dealing with fear is to look at what makes you feel afraid. Here are some things to consider:

+ Some people are afraid of the past. Their fear stems from old wounds that have not fully healed. You might be holding on to anger, guilt, shame, self-pity, or a sense of failure, which is like infected tissue trapped beneath an old scar. There is great value in getting the poison out of the wound. On a physical level, physicians would call it debridement, a process by which they cut away dead tissue to aid in healing. On a spiritual level, it is a process of reconciliation in which you let go of anger and resentment by forgiving yourself, your ex-spouse, and anyone else connected with the divorce.

+ Some people are afraid of the annulment process. They are afraid of having to talk to someone at the tribunal. They are afraid of being asked embarrassing questions. But people who have gone through the annulment process admit that the process seems more intimidating than it really is. Once they get started, their fears dissipate.

✦ Some people are afraid their case will be denied. There are no guarantees that you will be granted an annulment. If this is your fear, you have to look at the annulment process from a different perspective. Try to look at it more as a way of obtaining valuable insights into your life and achieving emotional and spiritual healing. These things can occur whether the annulment is granted or not.

✦ Some people are afraid of how others will react. They are afraid their ex-spouse or their children will be upset. They are afraid of what friends, neighbors, co-workers, or parishioners might say. Most of these fears evaporate when people begin to see annulments from a spiritual perspective as a process that leads to healing and closure.

It is important to share your fears with someone. Talk to your priest, deacon, or someone on the parish staff. In some dioceses, there are people who have been trained to provide spiritual and emotional support for someone who is applying for an annulment. When you receive sympathy, understanding, and reassurance from someone, fear begins to lose whatever power it had over you.

Staying positive

Once you've made the decision to proceed with the annulment process, don't be surprised if fear comes crashing back. Remind yourself that you've already dealt with those feelings. Say to yourself, *I am going to do this. I am not afraid.*

> Nothing in life is to be
> feared, only understood.
> — MARIE CURIE

Sometimes fear comes back disguised as doubts. You might hear a little voice inside saying, "You'll never be able to go through with this." Counteract doubts with positive thoughts. Say to yourself, *I am not going to doubt myself. I am not afraid.*

Sometimes fear comes back disguised as negativity. You might find yourself being critical of the people or procedures involved in the process. As negativity builds your imagination may run rampant. Before long you are sucked into a whirlpool of doubts and fear. Counteract negativity with positive thoughts: *I'm going to give this a chance. I am not afraid.*

Can a Person Who Receives an Annulment Become a Saint?

A Canadian diocese has opened an investigation into the possibility of sainthood for Catherine de Hueck Doherty (1896-1985), the founder of Madonna House, whose marriage to her first husband was declared invalid by the Church. In 1931, her spiritual director urged her to apply for an annulment after her husband's infidelities ended the marriage. The first tribunal agreed that the marriage should be annulled. A second tribunal disagreed, so the matter was sent to Rome. On March 17, 1943, the Supreme Sacred Congregation of the Holy Office in Rome decreed that the marriage was invalid. The following day, Pope Pius XII approved the decision and a decree of nullity was issued. On June 25, 1943, she married Edward Doherty in the private chapel of Bishop Bernard J. Sheil of Chicago. Her cause for canonization is currently under investigation.

Giving everything to God

God has promised that if we rely upon Him, we will be freed from fear. Psalm 46 assures us that "God is our refuge and our strength, a very present help in time of trouble. Therefore we will not fear . . ."

Giving our fears and our pain to God allows us to let them go. Letting go is the essence of authentic spirituality. It brings us to an attitude of peaceful acceptance.

+ If everything is in God's hands, we don't have to worry about anything.
+ If God is our strength, we will get help from Him to overcome fear and deal with pain.
+ If God is our ever-present help, we don't have to worry about being alone. God will be with us every step of the way.
+ If God is with us, we can believe, like St. Paul, that "in everything God works for good with those who love him" (Rom. 8:28).

> Do not be afraid . . . Let His power of truth and love enliven every aspect of your existence.
> — POPE JOHN PAUL II

The people who get the most out of the annulment process are the ones who approach it from a spiritual perspective. Whether or not the annulment is granted is often irrelevant because the process leads them into a closer relationship with God.

The Breathing Prayer

One of the prayers I teach people who are starting the annulment process is the breathing prayer. I ask them to breathe in God's love and breathe out fear; breathe in God's love and breathe out pain; breathe in God's love and breathe out anger and resentment; breathe in God's love and breathe out tension or anxiety; breathe in God's love and breathe out anything that is not of God.

This prayer calms you down when you feel negative emotions building. It helps you fall asleep if your mind is racing. It assures you that God is filling you with love. It brings you to a deeper understanding of what St. John meant when he wrote "perfect love casts out fear" (1 Jn. 4:18).

Perhaps the best advice comes from St. Francis de Sales:

Do not look forward in fear to the changes of life;
Rather look to them with full hope that as they arise,
God, whose very own you are, will lead you safely through all things.
And when you cannot stand it, God will carry you in His arms.
Do not fear what may happen tomorrow;
The same everlasting Father who cares for you today
will take care of you today and every day.
He will either shield you from suffering or will give you
unfailing strength to bear it.
Be at peace and put aside all anxious thoughts and imaginings.

QUESTIONS FOR REFLECTION

1. What kind of poison is left in your old wounds?
2. What fears do you have about the annulment process?
3. In what way can you turn over your fears to God?

CHAPTER 3

Thinking It Through

"When I went through my divorce, I had to dredge up all the painful reasons our relationship deteriorated and our marriage failed," one woman admitted. "The annulment process is the opposite. It gives me the opportunity to go back in time and look at the person I was before I was married. It helped me realize that how I was raised, my unrealistic expectations, and my immaturity, all contributed to why I got involved with my ex-spouse in the first place!"

The questions the annulment process allows you to ponder are much different from what you may have asked yourself during the divorce:

✦ *Were we both trying to follow God's will? Or was there some other motivation for getting married?*

✦ *Did my ex-spouse and I really understand the true meaning of sacramental marriage?*

✦ *Did we bring to the marriage things from the past that made us incapable of making a lifelong commitment?*

I've met many people who expressed astonishment and relief that they would be taking this different approach. Many people felt as if they had been spiritually and emotionally mangled during the stark legalities of the divorce. They began to see the annulment process as a chance to wipe the slate clean. They began to see it as a positive approach that would lead to a new outlook toward life. They began to see it as a chance to deepen their relationship with God.

"I experienced extreme spiritual death during my divorce," one man told me. "The annulment process restored my faith in God and in the Catholic Church."

> "Let not your hearts be troubled; believe in God, believe also in me."
> — JN. 14:1
> ~€9%~

Before you begin

Set aside some quiet time when you can look back on the past in a prayerful way. In the quiet, you will hear different voices that draw you in different directions. It is important to distinguish between the voice of temptation, the voice of your own ego, and the voice of the Holy Spirit.

The voice of temptation will tell you about your faults, your failings, your limitations, your inability to move forward. The voice of your ego will taunt you about what other people will think and make you question why you should have to go through this. The voice of the Holy Spirit will be a quiet presence that will assure you that you are loved by God and something good will come from this.

✦ Ask the Holy Spirit to guide you as you look back in time.
✦ Ask for the wisdom to see clearly the truth about your own family or your spouse's family.
✦ Ask for the courage to look honestly at problem situations and painful realities.
✦ Ask for the grace to rise above anger or resentment.
✦ Ask for the ability to forgive and to seek forgiveness.
✦ Ask to be healed spiritually and emotionally.

Getting started

Read through each of the following sections slowly. After each section, close your eyes and think about the past. Keep a pen and notebook handy so you can jot down specific incidents or examples that come into your mind.

> The longest journey of any person is inward.
> — DAG HAMMARSKJOLD
> ❦

Don't try to rush through this process. You might want to go back through a section several times before you move on to the next section. Remember, you are on a journey into the past in an attempt to uncover and understand the truth.

Family of origin

When people decide to get married, they usually focus on their own relationship as a couple. But it's never just the two of you. When you marry, you unite yourself with someone who was raised in a family that had its own ideas, expectations, traditions, beliefs, and ways of doing things. You and your spouse bring all of your family issues and experiences into your relationship.

22

For example, the family of your ex-spouse may have been very different from yours, and you may have assumed that your ex-spouse would eventually become more like your family. Or you may have married someone who was raised in a family that was so similar to your family that you simply took for granted that you would agree on everything.

Neither of these assumptions is true.

When you begin to look at your own family and then look at your spouse's experience of growing up, you may see problem areas that never occurred to you. You may see factors that undermined your relationship. You may see that no matter how much chemistry there was in your relationship, the two of you were never destined to be together.

One way to begin this exploration is to ask yourself a few questions:

✦ What makes you feel uncomfortable when you think about your family of origin?

✦ What makes you feel uncomfortable when you think about your spouse's family?

✦ Did you choose your spouse because he or she was like one of your parents? Or did you choose your spouse because he or she was completely different?

✦ Was the decision to marry influenced by your desire or your spouse's desire to get away from family members?

When mature people enter into a valid marriage, they have to be willing to let go of attitudes, learned behaviors, and problems from the past. Each person must be willing to change. But this can only happen if both people are aware of how the past affected them.

> All human beings should try to learn before they die what they are running from, and to, and why.
> — JAMES THURBER

For example, it is not uncommon for the child of an alcoholic to marry someone who is destined to become an alcoholic because he or she learned as a child the patterns of behavior surrounding alcoholism. When alcoholism begins to manifest itself in the marriage, the person is usually shocked. Warning signs went unheeded because it was too familiar from his or her family experience.

Another red flag is how your ex-spouse related to your family members and friends. Maybe their relationships disturbed you, but you assumed that it would not affect your marriage. Maybe family members or friends advised you not to marry this person. What did they see that you could not see? Why didn't you believe them?

As part of the annulment process, you will have the chance to explore more deeply these kinds of family-of-origin issues. It will help you to determine whether you entered into the marriage with full maturity, full awareness, and full consent.

Why did you say "I do"?

The old saying "love is blind" has much truth in it. When you fall in love, you see the other person in a kind of glow that hides reality. You get swept up in a kind of romantic delirium that alters your judgment and stops the capacity for critical thinking. If you were married when this romantic intensity was in full force, you may have overlooked important indications that this marriage was not meant to be. You may have gotten married for the wrong reasons. Do you recall yourself saying things such as:

> *I finally found someone who will take care of me.*
> *This person will always make me happy.*
> *I won't be lonely anymore.*
> *This person will accept me just the way I am.*
> *We agree on everything. We never argue.*

There are also situations where people fall in love with the idea of marriage rather than the person they are marrying. They want the wedding, the honeymoon, the house, the cars, the kids. It's not long before reality crushes the unrealistic dreams that led you into what you expected to be a "perfect marriage."

> Nothing is easier than self-deceit. For what each man wishes, that he also believes to be true.
> — DEMOSTHENES

Courtship issues

How you and your ex-spouse treated each other during your courtship could have a bearing on the annulment process. Sometimes people are ashamed of things that happened. They hide the truth because of embarrassment or because they are trying to forget. But these kinds of experiences help the tribunal identify the attitudes that the spouses brought with them to the altar on the wedding day.

If there were instances of verbal, emotional, or physical abuse, it is important to acknowledge it. As painful as it might be, these kinds of behaviors are not in line with what the Catholic Church regards as an appropriate attitude toward marriage.

Another sensitive area is the sexual history of both you and your spouse. This is not intended as an intrusion into your personal life. The tribunal is looking for attitudes or behaviors that might not be in line with what the Church teaches about human sexuality.

Experiences of infidelity during courtship are important, especially if the infidelity continued into the marriage. It is impossible for someone to enter into a valid marriage if he or she maintains an emotional attachment to another person.

Identify examples of immaturity before marriage. It might include difficulty holding a job, problems managing money, unusual dependency on other people, reckless behavior, inappropriate risk-taking or inability to make a commitment.

Try to remember what expectations you had before marriage. Did you assume that marriage would make all of the bad things disappear? Did you assume your fiancé would change his or her mind about important issues such as having children? Did either of you enter the marriage with the idea that you would get divorced if everything didn't work out?

Addictions

Incidents of heavy drinking or drug usage during courtship are often preludes to serious addiction, but there is usually an assumption that this person will settle down after the marriage. In fact, the person was probably already in the early stages of addiction.

> Don't ever take a fence down until you know why it was put up.
> — G.K. CHESTERTON
>
>

Experts agree that addictions develop gradually. The cycle begins when a person starts to rely on a substance or a behavior to deaden emotional pain or physical discomfort. Over time, the person moves from reliance to addiction.

People suffering from addictions are incapable of a close, personal relationship with God or another person because the overwhelming dependency on an addictive substance takes over their lives. An addicted person acts in opposition to the most basic spiritual values. The addiction destroys the person's capacity for truth, self-discipline, and love.

If addiction posed a problem in your relationship, look for examples of genetic predisposition toward addictive behavior in the family of origin. Other factors could include environment, how someone handled negative situations, and a reduced ability to deal with physical, mental or emotional trauma.

Psychological problems

The mental and emotional states of a person are important in the annulment process. The Church recognizes that someone suffering from mental illness may be incapable of the duties and responsibilities required for a valid marriage.

> All truths are easy to understand once they are discovered; the point is to discover them.
>
> — GALILEO

If there is a history of bipolar disease, schizophrenia, personality disorders, or other mental instability, you may have grounds for an annulment. Sometimes, people with mental illnesses appear to function adequately at work or in the community, but are unable to offer the emotional stability needed to maintain a supportive and loving relationship with a spouse or with children. When you think back, you may recognize that there were warning signs, but for one reason or another, you did not realize the full implications.

Other things to consider

Were there times during your engagement when you or your ex-spouse wanted to break up or cancel the wedding? Was there pressure from family members or friends to go through with the wedding? Other things to consider include:

- **Fraud**
  Anytime a person represents himself or herself as someone other than who and what they are, there is the potential for fraud. If your relationship involved lies, deceit, or secrets, you did not really know the person you were marrying. If someone makes a promise to do something with no real intention to follow through on that promise, then it is not really a promise.

- **Problems during Marriage Preparation**
  Think about what happened when you met with the priest or attended Marriage Preparation sessions. Was there any reluctance on the part of your ex-spouse to be married in the Catholic Church? Did you have to convince him or her to participate in Marriage Preparation? Did you both understand what the Church

teaches about marriage? Did either of you disagree with what the Church teaches about human sexuality?

- **Problems on the wedding day**
  Did anything unusual or inappropriate happen? It is becoming increasingly common for a bride or a groom to drink alcohol or take drugs before the ceremony. Even if a person is not an addict, the influence of alcohol or drugs could make someone incapable of the rational thought needed to give full consent. It could be a sign of immaturity or an indication of a deep-seated unwillingness to go through with the wedding that had to be suppressed.

Recognizing the truth

As you to begin to recognize the truth about yourself and your ex-spouse, you may see problems on both sides. No matter what your ex-spouse believed or how your ex-spouse behaved, you may recognize that you were too immature in your own thinking to realize that this was not going to be a valid marriage. You may look back and say to yourself, "*I should have known better! I never should have gone through with it.*"

> We shall not cease from exploration,
> And the end of all our exploring
> Will be to arrive where we started
> And know the place for the first time.
> — T.S. ELIOT

The annulment process will be your opportunity to correct mistakes you made in the past. The new insights that you obtain as you think about the past will be a tremendous help as you enter the annulment process. But don't be surprised if these new insights into the past also unleash feelings of anger or resentment.

QUESTIONS FOR REFLECTION

1. In what ways do you see the annulment process as being different from your divorce?
2. What are some of the personal issues that affected your decision to marry?
3. What warning signs did you miss?

Dealing with Resentments

"I thought I had let go of anger and resentment from my divorce," one man told me. "I was surprised when those feelings came crashing back during the annulment process."

Everyone's experience of divorce is different. It is not unusual for the initiator of the divorce to experience a mixture of fear, relief, doubt, and guilt. The other spouse is more likely to experience shock, betrayal, anger, abandonment, and desire for revenge. Eventually, both parties come to some level of acceptance that the marriage is over. But resentments that formed on both sides during the breakup can take root in the soul.

> We are hard-hearted and close-minded for years. Then comes a moment of vulnerability and mercy. We break down and break through.
> — RICHARD ROHR, O.F.M.

While the annulment process is often a trigger for bringing old resentments back to life, it also gives you a chance to deal with those resentments on a spiritual level. It gives you the opportunity to understand what kind of resentment you're holding on to, how it affects you, and how you can let go of resentment.

"I buried a lot of resentments — not just toward my ex-spouse, but toward my parents, family members, and friends for the way they reacted to my decision to end the marriage," one woman admitted.

"The annulment process really helped me get beyond anger and resentment," another woman explained. "I feel as if I have been liberated."

What is resentment?

Resentment is anger at yourself or someone else that has been buried deep inside. The original anger may have been justified. What happened may have been wrong or unfair. But instead of dealing with the anger, it was tucked away where it was allowed to linger as resentment.

When you are resentful, you hold on to the pain. You feel sorry for yourself. You feel bitter. You may suffer from nightmares or insomnia. You may tense your jaw or grit your teeth. You may become so consumed with resentment that you have a hard time finding joy in the present moment. You become a prisoner of your own negativity.

You can hold onto resentment forever. But carrying resentment is a heavy burden. In the end, the person who suffers the most from your resentment is you!

> To forgive is to set a prisoner free and discover that the prisoner was you.
> — LEWIS B. SMEDES

Getting rid of resentments

The first step in getting rid of resentment is to recognize what it is that makes you feel resentful.

- *What caused feelings of resentment to surface in you?*
- *Do your resentments stem from your childhood? Your family relationships?*
- *Are you resentful toward your ex-spouse? Your children?*
- *Do you feel as if someone deliberately intended to hurt you?*
- *Were there other factors involved that were beyond everyone's control?*
- *Is there another way that you could look at what happened?*
- *Is there a missing piece that might help you see a bigger picture?*

As you begin to recognize the cause of your resentment, you may uncover layers of attitudes or influences from the past that feed into your resentments.

"I grew up in a very unforgiving family," one man told me. "There was a lot of anger in our house and a lot of blaming. I can see now that I carried all of that into my marriage and then passed it on to my children. It was like a big cycle of anger and resentment that never got resolved."

> You must be emptied of that wherewith you are full, that you may be filled with that whereof you are empty.
> — ST. AUGUSTINE

Learning to let go

The best way to let go of resentments is to forgive. When you forgive, you make a clear, free decision to let go of the resentment and the pain. You may not feel like forgiving. The people who hurt you may not deserve your forgiveness. They might not want your forgiveness. But you choose to forgive because forgiveness is good for you. Forgiveness frees you. It releases feelings of anger, resentment, hatred, frustration and revenge.

Throughout the Gospels, Jesus tells us to forgive. He warns that we cannot expect to be forgiven for our own failings, if we can't forgive others.

> There is something divine about forgiveness. It is truly and closely aligned to charity, to love, to God himself.
> — CATHERINE DE HUECK DOHERTY

The problem is that it is not easy to forgive. It is not something that happens quickly. It's a good idea to incorporate your desire to forgive into a prayer. Tell God that you want to let go of resentment. Ask Jesus to walk back with you in time and free you from the pain.

Try standing before a crucifix and saying out loud:

Jesus, I forgive the people who have hurt me. Jesus, as you asked your Father to forgive the people who crucified you, I am asking you to forgive the people in my life who have hurt me.

The Sacrament of Reconciliation can help. Go to a priest and tell him that you've been holding onto resentment for a long time and you want to let it go.

It's a good idea to say an Our Father or a Hail Mary each time you think about the people who have hurt you. It will be a reminder to yourself and a sign to God that you are sincere in your desire to forgive.

Letting go of pain
Forgiving doesn't mean that you automatically forget everything that happened. It means that you choose not to hold onto painful memories. There is a difference between forgetting, which erases something from your mind, and choosing not to remember. The temptation to be angry or resentful may resurface, but you have to remind yourself that you've already made the decision to forgive. You have decided not to think about it.

> Regret is an appalling waste of energy; you can't build on it; it's only for wallowing in.
> — KATHERINE MANSFIELD

Forgiving yourself
Sometimes, the hardest person to forgive is yourself. You may struggle with guilt or regret over

things you said or did. You may chastise yourself for immaturity, stubbornness, selfishness, or the inability to understand; you may feel a deep sense of failure. But now is the time to let go of all that, to release it to the past where it belongs. Accept the fact that no one is perfect. Everyone makes mistakes. The Sacrament of Reconciliation can help you to reconcile your past and begin again with a clean slate. It gives you the opportunity to let go of shame, guilt, fear, and feelings of failure.

Spiritual healing

When you decide to let go of resentments, painful memories, and feelings of failure, you open yourself to the power of the Holy Spirit, who can heal you spiritually and emotionally. You feel God's presence in your life. You see new purpose in your life. You feel gratitude for all of the good things that are happening.

> "Peace I leave with you; my peace I give to you."
> — JN. 14: 27

"I told God that I wanted to forgive my parents, my ex-spouse, and everyone else who had hurt me," a woman admitted. "I kept praying and asking God to take away resentment. It didn't happen all at once, but gradually, I could feel God filling me with a deep inner peace that helped me to see things from a different perspective."

This deep inner peace is the essence of spiritual healing. It is the peace the world cannot give. It is a gift of grace from a loving God.

QUESTIONS FOR REFLECTION

1. What resentments surfaced as you began to look back on your life?
2. How have old resentments affected your life?
3. How are you going to deal with your resentments?

CHAPTER 5

Beginning the Annulment Process

You've decided to proceed. You've prayed for courage and understanding. You've looked into the past. You suspect that your marriage may have been invalid.

Call your parish office and ask for information on how to begin the annulment process. In some dioceses, you will be asked to make an appointment with your pastor or someone on the parish staff. This person will explain the process and give you the forms.

In other dioceses, you might be instructed to call the diocesan office that handles the annulment process. It may be called the Marriage Tribunal or the Office of Canonical Services.

People frequently ask if they have to initiate the annulment process in the diocese where they were married. If you live in a different diocese, you should call the local tribunal and ask what your options are. There are some situations in which a case can be opened in another diocese if proper permissions are obtained.

> To him who is
> determined it
> remains only to act.
> — ITALIAN PROVERB
>
> ~❦❧~

No matter where you begin the process, it's important to understand that the early stages of the annulment process are involved with collecting information.

"I was overwhelmed by the paperwork," one woman told me. "It wasn't until I sat down with a friend who had gone through the annulment process that I calmed down. She helped me break the process down into smaller steps and I began to see that I could do this!"

The paperwork

The packet that you receive contains information about the annulment process and guidelines for writing a personal history. Your written story is important because it forms the basis for determining whether or not you have grounds for an annulment. The guidelines for writing your story may be in the form of a questionnaire or they may be a list of categories with suggestions for what information to include in each section. Tribunals usually want you to submit no more than eight to ten typewritten pages.

You will also receive an application that will ask for your current religion, the date and place of your baptism, dates of marriage and civil divorce, names of family members or friends who will support your story, and the name and address of your ex-spouse.

A tribunal is bound by Canon Law to try and locate the ex-spouse so that he or she has a chance to respond. Your ex-spouse has the right to know what you have said. He or she has the right to offer additional witnesses. When a decision is made, your ex-spouse has the right to accept the decision or challenge it.

Some people get upset when they realize that their ex-spouse will be contacted. "I went through hell with that man," one woman told me. "I have an order of protection against him. If the tribunal contacts him, he will start thinking about me again, and he might come after me. I can't go through with this!"

> Do not anticipate trouble or worry about what may never happen.
> — BENJAMIN FRANKLIN

I always advise people not to abandon the process at this point. You will be able to discuss your situation with someone from the tribunal before anyone is contacted. The tribunal has experience in dealing with these kinds of situations and may be able to offer you the reassurance you need.

Writing your personal history

It's not easy to sit down and write. "I got hung up with the writing part," one man acknowledged. "Writing is not something that comes easily to me."

Some dioceses have volunteers who can help you with the paperwork. Some dioceses offer annulment retreats or annulment writing workshops, which are structured to assist you in writing your story.

"I had a lot to tell and I didn't know how to tell it," one woman admitted. "Working with an Annulment Companion helped me be concise and put my thoughts on paper. I don't know if I would have finished this on my own."

If you don't have access to this kind of help or if you'd rather write your narrative in the privacy of your own home, this chapter will provide the guidance that you need.

> Accept peacefully whatever you have to do and try to get things done
> in order. If you attempt to do everything all at once or without order,
> your mind will be frustrated and grow weary and you are likely to
> be overwhelmed by the pressure and accomplish nothing.
> — St. Francis de Sales

Putting it down on paper

Set aside specific time slots for writing your story. Some people set aside time on the weekend. Some people take an hour or two several evenings a week. Use whatever method of writing is most comfortable. Some prefer a computer. Some use a pad and pencil. Some like to write in a room that is quiet. Others need background music.

It might be easier to approach this as if you were filling out a questionnaire. In this chapter you will find a list of questions that will help you get started. Just write down your answers to the questions.

If writing is impossible, read the questions and then speak your answers into a tape recorder. You can transcribe the tape when you're finished.

As you respond to the questions, try to include examples. Don't write *My former spouse was immature* or *My former spouse was irresponsible.* Give specific examples of how your former spouse was immature or irresponsible. Include as many facts as possible. For example, you might write:

> *My former spouse was unfaithful twice before we were married, but each time he promised it was a mistake that would not happen again. I don't know why I believed him. After we were married, he had three affairs that I am aware of.*

As you write, refer to whatever notes you took when you first began to think back on what happened. Your goal at this point is to get a first draft of your story. As you work through the questions, skip the ones that don't apply. Don't worry about spelling or grammar. Don't worry about trying to find grounds for an annulment. The tribunal will determine if there are grounds based on what they read in your story. Just answer the questions and get as much information down on paper as possible. You can go back later and edit what you wrote.

> Writing itself is an act of faith, and nothing else.
> — E. B. White

Before you start writing, ask the Holy Spirit for inspiration, courage, and perseverance. Don't give in to the temptation to quit. You are seeking truth and justice.

Family background

The first time you go through these questions, write about your own family background and how you were raised. Then go through the questions again and write about the family background and experiences of your ex-spouse:

> Fill your paper with the breathings of your heart…
> — WILLIAM WORDSWORTH

+ Describe the character of your parents. Who was dominant? Did they get along? What was the extent of their education? What did they do for a living? Did your parents ever separate, divorce or remarry?
+ How did you get along with your parents? Your brothers and sisters?
+ Describe in detail any physical, emotional, or verbal abuse in your family.
+ Was there infidelity in your parents' marriage?
+ Describe any alcohol or drug abuse in your family.
+ Were there psychological problems?
+ Describe any unusual fears you had in childhood or later.
+ Did you make friends easily? Or were friendships a struggle?
+ How far did you go in school? How were your grades? Did you get along with teachers and peers?
+ How old were you when you went on your first date? Did you have any serious relationships, and if yes, why were they terminated? How were they terminated?
+ Outline a brief history of your sexual experiences. What were your attitudes toward sex? Did you have any problems in relation to your sexuality?
+ Describe family religious practices.
+ Did you have any unusual illnesses or other difficulties in childhood?
+ Did you have long-range goals or did you live for the moment?
+ Describe your work record including dependability and responsibility.
+ Did you save money or spend it impulsively?

- Evaluate the strong and weak areas of your personality. Are you quick tempered? Compassionate? Moody? Naïve? Jealous? Kind? Selfish? Ungrateful? Truthful?
- Do you act erratically or unpredictably? Do you use good judgment?

> If you do not tell the truth about yourself you cannot tell it about other people.
> — VIRGINIA WOOLF

Your courtship
- How did you meet? How long did you know each other before marriage?
- How long did you date before marriage? How often did you date? What did you do on dates?
- What was the major source of attraction?
- Where there any problems in dating? Any verbal, physical, or emotional abuse? Did you have break-ups during the relationship? Why?
- What was your attitude toward sex before marriage? What was your ex-spouse's attitude?
- How did the topic of marriage come up? How long were you engaged?
- What was your attitude toward the marriage? What did your family and friends think about you marrying this person?
- Was there any pressure to marry? Did either of you feel reluctant or doubtful about getting married? Did either of you see marriage as an escape? Was there an unexpected pregnancy before marriage?
- Were there any problems prior to the marriage?
- Was there any infidelity during the courtship? What was the attitude of each person toward fidelity, permanence of marriage, and divorce?
- Did either of you dislike children or not want to have children?
- Did you attend Pre-Cana sessions? Describe your attitudes and your spouse's attitudes toward the Pre-Cana. Was there anything presented in the sessions that one or both of you disagreed with?

Your wedding and honeymoon
- Describe any unusual events or behavior on the part of you or your former spouse at the wedding rehearsal or the rehearsal dinner.
- What did you think and how did you feel on your wedding day? Did you have second thoughts about getting married? Did someone have to persuade you to go through with the wedding?

- What did your former spouse think and feel on the day of the wedding? Did he or she have second thoughts about getting married? Did someone have to persuade your spouse to go through with it?
- Did you or your former spouse drink alcohol or use drugs in the hours before the wedding ceremony?
- What were your attitudes at the church and the reception?
- Were there any unusual incidents at the wedding or the reception?
- Was the marriage consummated? If not, why not?
- Were there any problems during the honeymoon?

> We must be true inside, true to ourselves, before we can know a truth that is outside us.
> — THOMAS MERTON
>

Your married life
- How long did the marriage last?
- Describe your affection for each other. Were there problems or disagreements over sex?
- Did either of you refuse to have children?
- What was the attitude of each partner toward responsibilities of married life (i.e. earning a living, housework, cooking, caring for children, home repairs, etc.)?
- Was there any physical, verbal, or emotional mistreatment?
- What role did each of your parents play in the marriage?
- What were the problems in the marriage? When did they arise?
- Was there abuse of money, alcohol, drugs, or gambling?
- Was there compulsive behavior in any form?

> We know the truth, not only by the reason, but also by the heart.
> — BLAISE PASCAL

- Were there any temporary separations? Give the cause and length of each separation. Describe the reasons and process of reconciliation, if any.
- What was the main reason for the final separation? What happened? Who filed for divorce?
- What is the marital status of each party since the divorce?

> The greatest loss that we all have to deal with is the loss of the image of ourselves as a perfect person.
> — FRED ROGERS

Counseling or therapy

Write down the names, addresses, dates, number of sessions, and diagnoses of any psychiatrists, psychologists, or therapists that either party may have had.

Editing your story

When you've finished answering the questions, blend your answers together into one long story. You can break up the text with subtitles such as "My Family Background," "My Spouse's Family Background," "Courtship," "Wedding," etc.

Now, put the papers aside for a week or two. You need distance so that you can go back and look at what you wrote with objectivity.

When you read through your story for the first time, remember that it is highly unlikely that someone could write a perfect first draft.

+ Some people write too much in the first draft. It's not unusual for people to write a sentence and then write a second sentence that says the exact same thing in other words. You might also find that you've used the same example more than once.
+ Other people don't write enough and have to add more details.

> If the only prayer you said in your whole life was, "thank you," that would suffice.
> — MEISTER ECKHART

Go through your story and make grammatical and spelling corrections. Ask yourself if what you wrote makes sense. Then, type or print out your story.

It's a good idea to have someone read it. Your parish priest, deacon, or pastoral associate might be willing. If they don't feel qualified, they can suggest someone else who can give you some feedback.

Once your history is finalized, you will probably experience a tremendous sense of relief. The painful parts of your past are no longer trapped inside of you. You have completed one of the most difficult parts of the annulment process. You might want to take a moment and thank God for guiding you along the way.

QUESTIONS FOR REFLECTION

1. How do you feel about writing your story?
2. Which part of your story is the most difficult to write?
3. When are the best times for you to write?

CHAPTER 6

Finding Witnesses

At one of our annulment information sessions, a young man sat quietly taking notes until the subject of witnesses arose. "I'd be embarrassed to ask family members and friends to testify," he said. "I don't understand why the tribunal needs witnesses!"

The tribunal needs witness to validate your story. They have to make sure that what you tell them about your background and the events leading up to your marriage is true. Witnesses also bring new information and insights to the case. It is all part of the process of gathering evidence.

Your witnesses must be people who knew you and your ex-spouse before your wedding day. The tribunal will want you to name at least two people. Some tribunals ask for four or five witnesses in case some of the people you name do not respond.

The credibility of the people you choose is important. It's a good idea to make a list of everyone you think might be helpful. You might want to include:

✦ Parents, siblings, or close relatives from your family and your ex-spouse's family.
✦ Family friends.
✦ Childhood friends.
✦ Classmates from grammar school, high school or college.
✦ The members of your wedding party.

We don't accomplish anything in this world alone . . . and whatever happens is the result of the whole tapestry of one's life and all the weavings of individual threads from one to another that creates something.

— SANDRA DAY O'CONNOR

- ✦ The priest or deacon who married you.
- ✦ The couple from the parish who conducted your Pre-Cana sessions.
- ✦ Physicians or counselors.
- ✦ Former employers or co-workers.
- ✦ Former teachers.

You can also name family members or friends who might not be able to testify to what happened before you were married but can serve as character witnesses and testify to your honesty and integrity.

Contacting witnesses

Ask these people if they will cooperate before you submit their names. Explain to them that you are investigating the possibility of a church annulment. Explain that the annulment process tries to determine whether both spouses were capable of entering into what the Catholic Church recognizes as a valid marriage. Let them know why you believe the marriage was not valid.

> Few things help an individual more than to place responsibility upon him, and to let him know that you trust him.
> — BOOKER T. WASHINGTON

You might have to answer questions about the annulment process and dispel misconceptions.

"When I called my sister to ask if she would be one of my witnesses, she laughed because she had told me right from the start not to marry my 'ex'," one man recalled. "I don't think she realized how much that hurt me. But she turned out to be the best witness I had."

What is expected

In most cases, witnesses never have to appear in person. The tribunal will send a questionnaire. Arrangements can be made to interview witnesses over the telephone if someone isn't comfortable with writing the answers. Witnesses will have to swear that their testimony is truthful.

The questions are not complicated:

- ✦ Describe the background of the man and woman. How did they relate to parents, siblings, or other relatives? Were there problems in the home?
- ✦ What were your impressions of the couple while they were dating? Were there any problems during courtship? Did family members and friends approve of this marriage? If not, why?

- Did anything unusual happen at the wedding ceremony? If yes, what?
- Did either party discuss whether they wanted to have children? Please explain.
- Before or during the marriage, were you aware of any difficulties related to jobs, finances, gambling, drinking, drugs, in-laws, religious beliefs, infidelity, abusive behavior (physical, sexual, mental, emotional), difficulty coping with ordinary problems? When in the marriage did you notice these things? Please give specific examples.

"I was more than willing to cooperate," one mother told me. "I didn't have to appear at the tribunal. All the paperwork was done in another city. They sent me a questionnaire. I filled it out and sent it back. I just told the truth."

> In a moment of decision, the best thing you can do is the right thing to do.
> — THEODORE ROOSEVELT

Encourage your witnesses to think about the process as gathering information and offering examples. Explain that this is not about blame.

"I never blamed either person," one witness recalled. "I said there was immaturity on both parts. Throughout every question, I repeated that I thought they were immature and that neither was prepared for marriage. They were attracted to each other, but they had no idea what it meant to be married. If two people are not mature, how can they commit themselves for the rest of their lives? Blame has nothing to do with it."

"I was glad that I could help," another witness admitted. "There were so many problems in their relationship that I felt that it was my responsibility to say something."

Don't take anything for granted

Sometimes, people you assume will be the most helpful may be the most reluctant. I had to intercede for one man who named his sister as a witness. She was a fallen-away Catholic and refused to cooperate because she felt that the Catholic Church had no right "to pry into someone's private business."

"Do you care about your brother?" I asked.

"Yes," she insisted.

"The Church isn't forcing your brother to do this," I explained. "This is something he wants to do. It's important to him. If you care about your brother, you will answer the questions."

I was surprised when she admitted that she didn't know what to say. I asked if she wanted me to go through the questions with her. When we finished, she thanked me.

Don't jump to conclusions

On the other hand, a person you might be hesitant to contact may become your best witness. One woman was afraid to ask her former mother-in-law to be a witness because she hadn't talked to her since the divorce.

"Do you think she might be helpful?" I asked.

"Yes," the woman replied. "She was the only one who really understood the situation, but I don't know if she'd be willing to answer questions."

I encouraged the young woman to ask. The mother-in-law ended up writing a ten-page letter to the tribunal with documentation that reinforced the fact that both her son and her former daughter-in-law did not have a sufficient level of maturity or understanding to make a lifelong commitment.

> The greatest difficulties lie where we are not looking for them.
> — JOHANN WOLFGANG VON GOETHE

When witnesses refuse

Sometimes witnesses refuse to cooperate because they are embarrassed or ashamed about what may have happened in the past. One mother was infuriated because her son revealed a history of mental illness on her side of the family. She refused to verify the information even though it was the truth.

Some people may be afraid that you or your former spouse will be upset at what they say. If one of your witnesses wants their testimony to be completely confidential, they can discuss their concerns with someone on the tribunal staff.

Reassure your witnesses. Tell them this is a matter of truth and justice. Encourage them to submit their paperwork as soon as possible. One of the major causes of delay in the annulment process is waiting for the testimony of witnesses. The time you spend lining up witnesses, explaining the process, and assuring them that their testimony is important is time well spent.

If you can't find witnesses

Sometimes, people have trouble finding witnesses. It is not unusual for elderly people to have difficulty finding witnesses:

Talking to Your Children

Before you begin to line up witnesses, it is important to tell your children that you are planning to seek a church annulment. It helps if you approach it as an opportunity to teach your children more about their Catholic faith.

The ages of your children will dictate how much you tell them. With younger children, you might just say that you are going to ask the Church to help you understand whether your marriage was a sacrament.

With older children you have the opportunity to explain to them what a sacramental marriage is supposed to be. You may want to offer some examples of how your marriage differed from the marriages of other family members that reflect more clearly what the Church teaches about the Sacrament of Matrimony.

The children may be concerned about how the annulment will affect them. Assure them that the civil marriage assures their legitimacy and that the Church annulment will not affect custody, child support or other legal matters.

They may want to know what to say if other people ask them about the annulment. Give them simple statements, such as, "My parents were not mature enough when they were married so it was not a sacrament."

With adult children, you can be more open. They will have many of the same concerns, but they will also have the capacity to understand more fully the reasons that you are seeking an annulment.

No matter what age your children are, throughout your conversation, assure them that they can ask you questions about the process at any time. Help them to understand that what you are doing is intended to be a healing process that will help everyone in the family put the pain of the divorce behind them.

- One woman told me that her parents and her two sisters would have been her only witnesses, but they had all died.
- A man rattled off a long list of family members, friends, and neighbors who had died.

Sometimes, people lose contact with members of the wedding party. They may succeed in locating male friends through the Internet, but it is often difficult to find women friends who have remarried and changed their names.

One man who was married by an Army chaplain during the Vietnam war had difficulty finding witnesses because his wife's family had dispersed, his own family had never met the bride, the army chaplain had died, and he could not find any of his army buddies.

If witnesses are a problem for you, don't give up. The tribunal may be able to help you locate people or identify witnesses that you might not have considered.

> Facts are stubborn things; and whatever may be our wishes, our inclinations, or the dictates of our passions, they cannot alter the state of facts and evidence.
> — JOHN ADAMS

Finalizing your paperwork

Once you have completed the application form, finished writing your story, and lined up witnesses, you should be ready to submit your paperwork to the tribunal. Some dioceses require that you show everything to your pastor before submitting it. In other dioceses you can submit the paperwork directly.

It's a good idea to make an extra copy of your paperwork before submitting it. You've already put a lot of work into this process. Don't take any chances that your paperwork might be lost.

Within a short time after submitting your paperwork, you will receive a letter from the tribunal asking you to call and make an appointment for

> Most of the important things in the world have been accomplished by people who have kept on trying when there seemed to be no hope at all.
> — DALE CARNEGIE

a preliminary interview. Most tribunals have extended hours in the evenings or on Saturdays.

Don't be nervous. Think of it as taking the next step in the process. Remind yourself that everything will be all right if you just go through this one step at a time.

A good prayer for this stage of the process is the Prayer of St. Ignatius of Loyola:

O Christ Jesus, when all is darkness, and I feel my weakness and help-lessness, give me the sense of your presence, your love, and your strength. Help me to have perfect trust in your protecting love and strengthening power, so that nothing may frighten or worry me, for, living close to you, I shall see your hand, your purpose, your will through all things.

QUESTIONS FOR REFLECTION

1. Who could you ask to serve as witnesses?
2. How will you explain the annulment process to your witnesses?
3. What will you do if your witnesses refuse to cooperate?

CHAPTER 7

Going to the Tribunal

Part of the anxiety people experience before their preliminary interview is that they don't know what to expect. Even the word "tribunal" sounds ominous. But you will find that it is just an administrative center with a waiting room, a receptionist, secretaries, conference rooms, and offices. The office staff is trained to answer your questions and assist you. Staff members may include lay people, priests, deacons, and religious sisters.

The preliminary interview
During your preliminary interview, the person assigned to your case will have a copy of the paperwork that you sent. You will meet in a private area. The tribunal staff member will ask you questions about the information you have submitted. He or she may invite you to explain a specific incident in more detail or to provide more information about your family situation, your courtship, your wedding day, or about your ex-spouse's family. The purpose of this questioning is to determine possible grounds for the annulment.

You may have assumed that you had grounds in a specific area, and you may have structured your written narrative to support those grounds. But the tribunal staff member may see something in your story that would make it easier to pursue the annulment on different grounds.

> Never assume the obvious is true.
> — WILLIAM SAFIRE
> ~⅊~

For example, I was working with a woman who assumed the grounds would center on her ex-spouse's emotional abuse and inability to make a commitment. During the preliminary interview, however, the tribunal staff member suggested that it might be better for her to establish grounds against herself for immaturity and lack of discretion.

"At first, I was shocked," the woman later recalled. "Why should the grounds focus on me, when he was the problem? Then, I began to see the bigger picture. I was only nineteen years old. I didn't understand what I was getting into. He was older and very controlling. He manipulated me and destroyed my self-esteem. He never really loved me. He controlled me. I finally saw that it was easier to admit that I was too young and immature — which was true — than it would be to establish grounds against him."

Additional paperwork

During the preliminary interview, you will be told that you will have to obtain copies of your marriage certificate and your civil divorce decree. The tribunal cannot begin the annulment process until your divorce is finalized

You will also be asked to obtain a current baptismal certificate for yourself and your ex-spouse. The Catholic Church is structured so that all of your sacramental information is kept at the parish of your baptism. On the back of your baptismal certificate, you will see a recap of when you received different sacraments — including information about your marriage. If you are granted an annulment, the tribunal will notify the parish of your baptism so the records will show that your marriage has been annulled.

Professional reports

If you underwent psychological counseling before, during, or after your marriage, the tribunal staff member may request that you sign a paper authorizing the release of records. You will also be told that there may be circumstances where the tribunal would ask you or your ex-spouse to speak to one of their counselors.

> Truth never hurts
> the teller.
> — ROBERT BROWNING

Witnesses

The tribunal staff person will ask about your witnesses. In case of a falling-out among family members, or family secrets that might impact the testimony of witnesses, it is important to let the tribunal staff member know. Tell the truth. You're not going to shock the tribunal staff member with anything you say. If you've had trouble finding witnesses, this is the time to explain.

Your former spouse

You will be told that the tribunal will try to locate your ex-spouse. In order to determine the facts of the case, the tribunal needs to hear both sides. You are considered "the petitioner" because you petitioned the tribunal to investigate the case. Your ex-spouse is considered "the respondent" because he or she has a right in Canon Law to respond.

If you don't know where your ex-spouse lives, the tribunal may ask for your help in locating family members or friends who might have a current address. Throughout the process, you will never be required to have direct contact with your ex-spouse. If you have a good relationship with your ex-spouse, you might want to explain to him or her in advance that you are pursuing an annulment, or you might decide that it is best to let the tribunal handle it.

A letter will be sent to your ex-spouse saying that you have asked the tribunal to look into the possibility of obtaining a Church annulment. Your former spouse will be assured that the tribunal is not questioning the validity of your civil union or the legitimacy of your children, but will look at whether the marriage took place in accord with what the Church teaches regarding the Sacrament of Matrimony.

Some tribunals send the ex-spouse a questionnaire. Some invite your ex-spouse to come to the tribunal for a personal interview. At this point, your ex-spouse has three choices:

> Because a thing seems difficult for you, do not think it is impossible . . . Whatever is possible for another, believe that you, too, are capable of it.
> — MARCUS AURELIUS

- ✦ He or she can cooperate.
- ✦ He or she can oppose the process.
- ✦ He or she can ignore the process and do nothing.

The best of all possible situations is when the ex-spouse cooperates. One woman told me: "My ex-husband's parents would not cooperate, but he did. All the stories were so close that someone at the tribunal asked if I had shown my papers to him, which I hadn't. In fact, my ex-husband added things that I didn't even know about that supported the case!"

There are, however, situations in which the ex-spouse tries to fight the process.

- ✦ Sometimes, the opposition stems from bitterness or a desire for revenge.
- ✦ Sometimes, the opposition stems from misconceptions, such as the erroneous belief that the annulment means the Church is saying a marriage never existed or that the annulment will make the children illegitimate.
- ✦ Sometimes, the opposition is related to "family secrets," such as a history of psychological problems, alcoholism, abuse, or homosexuality.

✦ Sometimes, one of the spouses sincerely believes that the marriage was valid and does not want the Church to issue a decree of nullity.

If you suspect that your ex-spouse will try to fight the process, it's best to be honest with the tribunal staff member. The tribunal is experienced in dealing with controversy. They can sort through the testimony and recognize when people are trying to alter the truth or manipulate the situation. Vindictive people lose credibility by their own negative actions.

"My ex-wife was so bitter that her testimony actually became like another witness to support my side of the story," one man recalled. "The tribunal caught her and her family members in lies."

> I think we may safely trust a good deal more than we do.
> — HENRY DAVID THOREAU

It is important to let the tribunal know if there is a history of violence or if you have a court order of protection against your ex-spouse. They have procedures for dealing with these kinds of situations.

If the tribunal cannot locate your ex-spouse, or if your ex-spouse does not respond to the tribunal's invitation to participate in the process within a specified time period, he or she can be declared absent and the case can proceed.

Confidentiality

Tribunal staff members are bound by confidentiality. They cannot discuss your case with anyone outside the tribunal. Your parish priest, your family members, friends, and witnesses will not be allowed to see your paperwork. You and your ex-spouse are the only ones allowed to read the file, and even you will not be allowed to remove documents or make photocopies.

Leaving the tribunal

Most people tell me that after their preliminary interview, they leave the tribunal with a sense of relief. The hard work of soul-searching, writing, and explaining is done. Now, the tribunal begins its part of the investigation. How long the investigation takes is influenced by several factors:

✦ The number of cases the tribunal is processing.
✦ How long it takes for your ex-spouse to respond to the tribunal's letters.
✦ How long your witnesses take in responding.
✦ How long it takes for medical records or reports to be sent to the tribunal.

✦ How promptly you return telephone calls and schedule appointments.

It's a good idea to call the tribunal once a month to ask about the status of your case. They will tell you if they are still waiting for witnesses or other paperwork. You might be able to prod people into responding more quickly.

While you wait

For many people, the most difficult part of the next few months is waiting. We live in a culture that expects instant results. We want to make things happen. We want to get things done. Waiting is almost always seen as something negative; it frustrates us — or tempts us to worry about whether things will turn out the way we want them to turn out.

But you always have a choice: You can allow this time of waiting to be a burden, or you can use this time to grow spiritually. It's all in the attitude you take.

Suppose, for example, that you began to think of waiting as a spiritual opportunity during which you will receive important gifts. Some of those gifts might include:

> Trust in the slow
> work of God.
> — Pierre Teilhard
> de Chardin

✦ The gift of patience
✦ The gift of appreciating the present moment
✦ The gift of hope
✦ The gift of humility
✦ The gift of gratitude
✦ The gift of humor and the ability to laugh at yourself
✦ The gift of trust in God
✦ The gift of deeper faith

While you are waiting, take some time to meditate on these gifts. Ask God to instill in you a peaceful sense of acceptance. St. Francis de Sales offers the following advice:

Let's not waste time in willing and wishing for things, but let God arrange them. We should "cast all our care upon him, since he cares for us," as the apostle Peter says. And note that he says, "all our care," that is, our concern about what comes to us from events of life as well as what comes to us from what we want or don't want. "He will take care" of the success of these things and he wishes for us whatever is best.

QUESTIONS FOR REFLECTION

1. What are your concerns about going to the tribunal?
2. How do you feel about the tribunal contacting your ex-spouse?
3. How will you deal with the time you spend waiting for the next stage of the process?

The Formal Process

When all the information is processed, the testimony is gathered from witnesses, and the paperwork is complete, the tribunal staff will review your case and decide whether or not you have grounds for an annulment. At this point you will receive another letter from the tribunal accepting or rejecting your case.

If your case is rejected

If the tribunal staff does not think that you have sufficient grounds, you will be told that the tribunal will not pursue the preliminary case any further. You will be advised that you can reopen your case if additional information or witnesses arise.

This is done for your protection. If the tribunal took your case to the formal stage without sufficient grounds, and the annulment was denied, you would not be able to reopen the case on the same grounds.

If your preliminary case is rejected, it's a good idea to ask for a meeting with someone at the tribunal to explain what happened. Cases involving foreign brides, migrant workers, multiple marriages, and elderly people are sometimes problematic because there are no living witnesses or access to documentation. The tribunal might want to believe your story, but in order to justify the case, there has to be proof.

I worked with one man whose ex-spouse had convinced his witnesses that testifying on his behalf would make the children illegitimate. She threatened to not let his relatives see the children if they cooperated. The tribunal could not proceed without witnesses. He decided that it was not worth trying to challenge his ex-spouse at this time.

Another man gave up on the process because all of the witnesses had died. When he admitted that he and his new wife were living as brother and sister without sexual relations, he was advised to talk to his pastor because the Church allows people in that situation to receive Communion.

You may be upset with the tribunal's inability to determine grounds, but it is always worth the time and effort to ask for clarification. There may be other avenues for you to pursue.

If your case is accepted

If the tribunal determines that sufficient grounds exist, you will be invited to move into the formal stage of the process. Your case will be assigned to a tribunal judge. You will be told what the grounds will be. If you don't understand what the grounds mean, it is important to ask for clarification because you will be expected to sign the formal petition agreeing to those grounds.

> Wisdom in life may perhaps consist in asking on all occasions: Why?
>
> — HONORE DE BALZAC

If you haven't brought your baptismal certificate and copies of your marriage certificate and divorce decree, you will have to make them available to the tribunal.

You will also be notified of the amount of the processing fee and when you are expected to pay it. Installment payments can be arranged. If you are having financial difficulties, please let the tribunal staff know about your situation. No one is ever denied an annulment because of inability to pay the processing fee.

Your formal hearing

Once the petition is signed, a formal hearing will be scheduled. This hearing is not like a courtroom session. You will meet with the judge assigned to your case and a staff member, who will serve as a notary. The purpose of

What Percentage of Annulments Is Granted?

In the United States, it is estimated that ninety percent of the petitions presented in the formal annulment process are approved. This is primarily due to the prescreening process in which tribunals only accept cases that have solid grounds. The tribunal staff will not recommend that a case be presented for a formal hearing unless they are fairly certain that the case will receive an affirmative decision.

this hearing is to make sure everything is documented. The judge will lead you through the process. A tape recorder may be running. You may be asked a few questions, but the process is not confrontational. You will formally agree to the grounds for the annulment. You will sign some papers.

"I was amazed at how kind and helpful the judge was," one man admitted. "He led me through, step by step. It wasn't a bad experience at all."

> Act as if what you
> do makes a
> difference. It does.
> — WILLIAM JAMES

Your ex-spouse's hearing
Your ex-spouse will also be invited to meet with one of the judges for this formal stage of the process, but the meetings can be arranged separately. If your ex-spouse decides not to attend the session, it is not a problem. The process will proceed without him or her. If your ex-spouse is opposed to the process, the formal opposition will be officially recorded at this time.

Your review
After the formal hearing, your case will be reviewed by several other people from the tribunal:

+ There is an advocate assigned to represent you.
+ There is a Defender of the Bond, who makes sure that there is sufficient reason to annul the marriage.
+ There is an advocate for your former spouse.

It is unlikely that you will meet these people. They will read through the testimonies and evidence presented by you, your ex-spouse, and your witnesses. They will each render an opinion. The judge assigned to your case will render a decision based on these opinions, the evidence, and the terms of Canon Law. It could take several months before you hear anything.

+ If it is decided that your marriage should not be annulled, you will be notified.
+ If it is decided that your marriage should be annulled, your case will automatically be sent to another tribunal for a second opinion. If the second court agrees, you will be issued a decree of nullity.
+ If the second court disagrees with the first, the case can be sent to the Roman Rota, which is the highest court of appeal in the Vatican, for a final determination.

When restrictions are placed

Most people don't realize that obtaining a decree of nullity does not automatically allow you to marry again in the Catholic Church. There are cases where the judges express serious doubt that one or both people are capable of entering into a sacramental union in the way that the Church understands marriage. In these situations, a restriction, which is called a *vetitum*, is placed on the decree. This requires that one or both of the persons must consult the tribunal and, in some cases, undergo counseling before they can be married in a Catholic Church.

> All human wisdom is summed up in two words — wait and hope.
> — ALEXANDRE DUMAS

"I was so angry when I saw that restriction," one man recalled, "but my wife calmed me down. She told me that counseling wouldn't hurt us, and it may make our relationship stronger and help us deal better with both sets of kids. We did six months of counseling, and then we were cleared to have our marriage convalidated. My wife was right. It helped in ways that I never anticipated."

A good prayer of acceptance for people who are facing a restriction comes from St. Teresa of Ávila:

Lord, grant that I may always allow myself to be guided by You,
always follow Your plans, and perfectly accomplish Your Holy Will.
Grant that in all things, great and small, today and all the days of my
* life,*
I may do whatever You require of me.
Help me respond to the slightest prompting of Your Grace,
so that I may be Your trustworthy instrument for Your honor.
May Your Will be done in time and in eternity by me, in me, and
* through me.*

The decree of nullity

In most cases, you and your ex-spouse will be notified that the decree of nullity has been approved without any restrictions. You will be free to enter into a new marriage in the Catholic Church or have your existing marriage convalidated. While marriage is the reason that many people enter into the annulment process, the granting of an annulment has other implications for some people:

- For one woman, her husband's annulment meant she could be received into the Catholic Church at the Easter Vigil.
- For a middle-aged woman, it meant that she could enter a religious community.
- For a young man, it meant that he could enter the seminary.

I've discovered that there are as many different reactions to receiving a decree of nullity as there are annulments.

- Some people admitted that it was a difficult process, but that it was worthwhile.
- Some discover that their anger and resentment toward their former spouse has dissipated.
- Most people feel an overwhelming sense of gratitude and a deep sense of peace.

"It was like the Lord was telling me through the tribunal that what happened in the past was over and I could close that door without any sense of guilt or failure," one man said.

"I felt as if I made my way through the darkness and, suddenly, God's healing light was shining down on me," a woman recalled. "If I ever marry again, I will be much more aware of the sacramental nature of marriage."

A good prayer of gratitude is attributed to St. Catherine of Siena:

O tender Father, You gave me more, much more
than I ever thought to ask for.
Thank you, and again thank you, O Father,
for having granted my requests,
and for having granted those things
that I never realized I needed or sought.

QUESTIONS FOR REFLECTION

1. What would you do if the tribunal told you that you do not have sufficient grounds?
2. How would you feel if the tribunal required counseling before you were allowed to marry again in the Catholic Church?
3. What will you do if your annulment is granted?

Moving On with Your Life

When the people I've worked with receive their annulment, they usually call to share the good news.

✦ *"It's like having a root canal," one man joked. "You feel so much better when it's over!"*

✦ *"I felt so much love when I realized that the tribunal exists to provide for those of us who have made mistakes in our lives," another woman told me.*

✦ *"My mother keeps saying that the annulment helped her to achieve closure," a son admitted. "It helped her to be at peace with the past."*

✦ *"My fiancé was deserted by his ex-wife," another woman explained. "In order to marry me, he had to have his marriage of twenty years annulled. God used this process to help both of us understand what a Catholic marriage is really meant to be."*

After the initial excitement and feelings of relief, people usually have lots of questions. Here are some of the things people want to know:

• **Do I have to tell my parish priest that I received the annulment?**
   If your pastor knew that you were going through the process, it would be good to let him know the annulment was granted. The tribunal does not notify your current parish. The tribunal sends notification to the parish where you were baptized so that it can be recorded in your baptismal record.

• **Now that my annulment is granted, can I receive Communion?**
   If you were simply divorced and had not remarried outside the Church, there was no restriction on receiving Communion. If you are in a second marriage, you should wait until your marriage is convalidated before receiving Communion.

- **What should I tell other people?**

  You don't have to tell other people anything. It's no one else's business. If you want to let other people know, you can tell them that you petitioned the Church for an annulment and it was granted. You can decide how much detail you want to offer about the grounds for the annulment or the process. You might want to dispel some of the myths about annulments by letting people know that it did not cost thousands of dollars and that your children are not illegitimate.

- **My ex-spouse is upset about the annulment. How do I deal with that?**

  There probably isn't much that you can do to change your former spouse's mind. Don't do anything that will aggravate the anger. Try to separate yourself emotionally. Try to understand that the roots of the anger may stem from other issues that are related to your former marriage, your divorce, child custody arrangements, and whatever plans you may have to remarry. Accept the fact that your ex-spouse has a different opinion, but that personal opinions don't change the decision that was made by the tribunal.

  > You have not time to occupy your thoughts with that complacency or consideration of what others will think. Your business is simply, "What will my Father in Heaven think."
  > — St. Katharine Drexel

- **Does the annulment affect the terms of the civil divorce?**

  Alimony, child support, custody, visitation, and other legal obligations are not affected by the annulment process. Both parties have a moral and legal obligation to fulfill the terms of the civil divorce.

- **How do I deal with my children who are upset about the annulment?**

  Listen to your children's concerns. They may have been given incorrect information about how the decree of nullity affects them. They might, for instance, feel that the annulment was in some way saying your marriage never existed. They might see it as an attempt on your part to abandon their other parent or to retaliate against him or her. They might be concerned that the process would make them illegitimate. If you can't correct your children's misconceptions, schedule a meeting with your children and a priest, deacon, or

> The truth is that our finest moments are most likely to occur when we are feeling deeply uncomfortable. . . . For it is only in such moment, propelled by our discomfort, that we are likely to step out of our ruts and start searching for different ways or truer answers.
> — M. Scott Peck

pastoral associate to address the issues. Once the misconceptions are addressed, you can begin to initiate conversations with your children about what is expected when people enter into a sacramental marriage.

- **What do I have to do if a restriction was placed on the decree?**
Contact the tribunal to find out why there is a restriction and what you have to do if you want to remarry in the Catholic Church. In most cases, the tribunal will require counseling or — in cases of mental illness, abuse, or addiction — some kind of treatment. Many people discover that complying with the recommendations of the tribunal can change their lives dramatically: they begin to uncover the underlying causes of infidelity, addictions, anger, violence, low self-esteem, chronic depression, and other problems that made it impossible for them to commit to a sacramental marriage. In most cases, the restrictions are lifted after the conditions have been met. If there is serious doubt that a person is incapable of entering into a binding union, however, the restrictions will remain, and that person will not be allowed to marry in the Catholic Church.

- **How do I arrange to be married in the Church?**
Call your parish office. They will let you know what you have to do to reserve a date. You and your fiancé will have to attend marriage preparation classes and go through a marriage investigation. You will need current copies of your baptismal certificates. At some point, you will meet with the priest or deacon who will perform the ceremony. Many parishes have booklets with checklists and guidelines.

- **How do I have my current marriage recognized by the Church?**
The decree of nullity opens the door for having an existing marriage convalidated. Some choose a simple ceremony in which the couple

exchanges vows in front of two witnesses and a priest or deacon. Others have a more elaborate ceremony with a Mass and guests. To arrange for a convalidation, contact your parish. Some couples schedule their convalidation as quickly as possible. Others chose a special date. "We are going to have our convalidation on the anniversary of our civil marriage so we will never forget our anniversary," one couple told me.

- **What if my spouse refuses to go through another ceremony?**
  Sometimes, a non-Catholic spouse finds it difficult to understand why another ceremony is desired or even needed. If you are in this situation, talk to a priest or someone at the tribunal about the possibility of a "sanation." The word comes from the Latin phrase *sanatio in radice*, meaning "healing at the root," and the process allows for the convalidation of a marriage without the renewal of consent.

> All of life is a journey. Which paths we take, what we look back on, and what we look forward to is up to us. We determine our destination, what kind of road we will take to get there, and how happy we are when we get there.
> — Dag Hammarskjold

- **How can I help other people who are going through the annulment process?**
  One of the amazing things about spiritual healing is that it leaves people with a burning desire to reach out and help others. Ten years ago in my diocese, several people who had gone through the annulment process decided to offer Annulment Seminars. They would arrange for the use of a parish hall, invite one of the judges from the tribunal to speak, publicize the event, and welcome people with big smiles and lots of refreshments.

> A compassionate person says, "I am your brother; I am your sister; I am human, fragile and mortal, just like you. I am not scandalized by your tears, nor afraid of your pain. I too have wept. I too have felt pain."
> — Henri Nouwen

As people from the annulment seminars received annulments, they asked if they, too, could help. It wasn't long before they formed a group called Annulment Companions. Their Annulment Seminars evolved into Annulment Writing Workshops, where they actually set aside a whole weekend or a series of evenings to help people to write their marital histories.

If you would like to get involved in a ministry that reaches out to others going through the annulment process, ask someone at the tribunal if there is a program in your diocese that already exists. If yes, call and volunteer.

If there is no program, consider starting one. It may be just the kind of encouragement that someone needs to begin the process of spiritual healing after a divorce.

> What once seemed such a curse has become a blessing. All the agony that threatened to destroy my life now seems like the fertile ground for greater trust, stronger hope, and deeper love.
> — HENRI NOUWEN

Where will you go from here?

The decision to begin the annulment process is a momentous step. What you learn from the process could change the course of your life and the lives of people you love.

There is no question that the process can be painful, but your former marriage was also painful, and the circumstances surrounding that marriage may have made it impossible for you to follow God's plan. The annulment process may offer a new way for you to follow God's will. It may allow the Holy Spirit to lead you along paths that you never knew existed and bring you to a far deeper sense of peace than you ever knew before.

QUESTIONS FOR REFLECTION

1. What other questions do you have about the annulment process?
2. What concerns do you have about the reaction of family members and friends?
3. In what ways do you see the annulment process as a way of following God's will?

C all your diocesan tribunal to find out what kind of assistance is available for people seeking annulments. There may be programs available that offer individual assistance. There may be annulment information sessions or annulment writing workshops. Help may be just a phone call away.

Books

Lorene Hanley Duquin, *They Called Her the Baroness: The Life of Catherine de Hueck Doherty*. New York, NY: Alba House, 1995.

Kay Flowers, Dennis Flowers, *Catholic Annulment, Spiritual Healing* (paperback). Liguori, MO: Liguori Press, 2002.

Michael Smith Foster, *Annulment: The Wedding That Was: How the Church Can Declare a Marriage Null* (paperback). Mahwah, NJ: Paulist Press, 1999.

Edward N. Peters, *Annulments and the Catholic Church: Straight Answers To Tough Questions*. West Chester, PA: Ascension Press, 2004.

Joseph P. Zwack, *Annulment: Your Chance to Remarry Within the Catholic Church: A Step-by-Step Guide Using the New Code of Canon Law*. New York, NY: Harper-San Francisco (Harper Collins), 1983.

Web Sites

Check your diocesan Web site for information about annulments. Many dioceses have guidelines for the annulment process posted, and some allow you to download the necessary forms.